ICE AGE
FACTS AND INFORMATION
ENVIRONMENT BOOKS

Children's Environment Books

BABY PROFESSOR
EDUCATION KIDS

Speedy Publishing LLC
40 E. Main St. #1156
Newark, DE 19711
www.speedypublishing.com

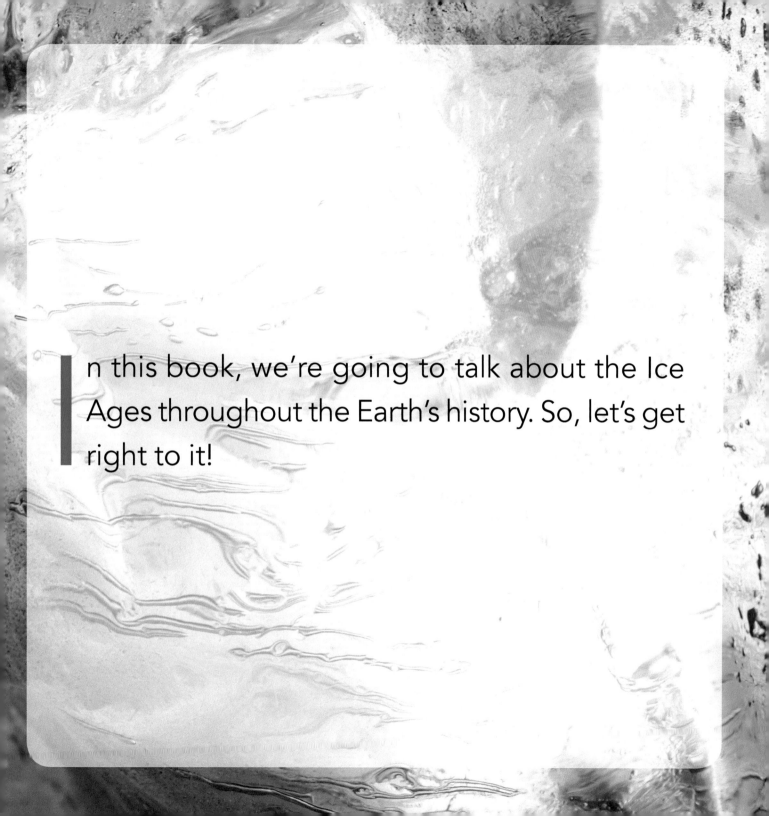

In this book, we're going to talk about the Ice Ages throughout the Earth's history. So, let's get right to it!

Snowy winter landscape at Pingvellir, Southern Iceland.

WHAT IS AN ICE AGE?

An Ice Age is a huge period of time in Earth's history when, compared to other time periods, the Earth's atmosphere and surface is colder. It's due to the decrease in temperatures worldwide. During these time periods, extensive sheets of ice appear in both hemispheres, north and south. Currently, there are ice sheets over Greenland in the northern hemisphere and over Antarctica in the southern hemisphere, so we're in an Ice Age right now.

However, in this Ice Age, the colder temperatures peaked around 20,000 years ago when regions of North America as well as large sections of land in Northern Europe were covered with glaciers and ice fields. During the peak of the current Ice Age, large animals like the wooly mammoths began to die out, but humans adapted to the colder conditions and survived.

Woolly Mammoth Family.

Ice age landscape from Iceland

HOW DOES AN ICE AGE BEGIN?

When the temperature around the world drops even by a few degrees over a long period of time it means that snow doesn't melt fully in certain regions. More snow falls on top of the layer that is already there. The bottom layer eventually turns to ice. Eventually, these layers of piled-up snow and ice become a glacier. The weight of the frozen mass of ice causes the glacier to move forward very slowly over landmasses.

Glaciers are very powerful and they cause massive changes to the surface of the Earth. Their movement gathers rocks as well as soil. Their weight is so heavy that they cause erosion and crush the Earth's surface. As the temperature continues to drop, plant and animal populations that thrive in cold weather are pushed to more southern landmasses. More ice forms and the sea levels drop dramatically.

Ice age.

This process makes it possible for rivers to create valleys that are deeper. Enormous lakes form inland. Land that was submerged underwater before is now exposed, creating bridges of land joining one continent to the next.

When the Ice Age retreats, the glaciers leave ridges of rocks and sediments. New lakes are created when the glaciers melt.

Ancient glacier

GLACIAL AND INTERGLACIAL PERIODS

Even within an Ice Age there are periods of time that are colder than others.

The colder time period within the Ice Age is called a glacial period. During this time, glaciers and ice sheets are expanding over landmasses.

The warmer time period within an Ice Age is called an interglacial period. During this time, the glaciers are beginning to melt, but there are still ice sheets over some landmasses.

Glacier Perito Moreno National Park in Argentina, Patagonia.

Winter Lake Huron

FIVE MAJOR
ICE AGES

The Earth has been around for over 4.5 billion years, but its early history was very, very hot. Scientists believe that there have been five major Ice Ages since the Earth was formed. Over the last one million years, there have also been about a dozen time periods where expansion of glaciers occurred.

The Huronian Ice Age

The first Ice Age on Earth has been identified as the Huronian Ice Age. After studying the geologic evidence from rocks, scientists believe that there was a decrease in the number of volcanic eruptions on Earth during this time period. Because there was less carbon dioxide in the air than there had been before, the Earth was plunged into an Ice Age that began 2400 million years ago and lasted for about 300 million years.

Boulders in ice age.

The Cryogenian Ice Age

Scientists call the second Ice Age the Cryogenian Ice Age. This Ice Age began about 850 million years ago and lasted for about 215 million years. Scientists believe the ice sheets during this time extended all the way to the equator. If astronauts could have seen it from space, they would have thought the Earth looked like a big snowball.

Glacial grooves in granite bedrock, legacy of the ice age.

The Andean-Saharan Ice Age

The third Ice Age, called the Andean-Saharan Ice Age, began about 460 million years ago and lasted for 30 million years.

Glacier.

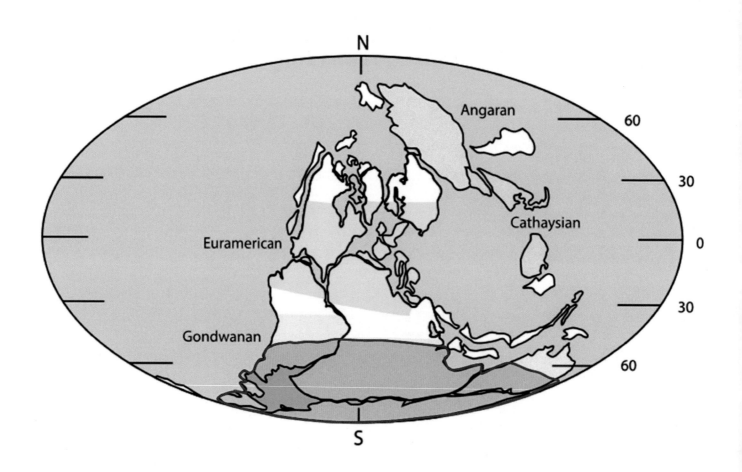

The Karoo Ice Age

The fourth Ice Age, called the Karoo Ice Age began 360 million years ago and lasted about 100 million years. It's named after geologic formations called glacial tills that are located in Karoo, South Africa. When you think of the continent of Africa, you often think of very hot deserts, but the climate there wasn't always that way. During past time periods, it was covered with ice. The glacial tills located there are the sediments that were left over by the movements of glaciers.

Approximate extent of the Karoo Glaciation (in blue), over the Gondwana supercontinent.

THE QUATERNARY ICE AGE

The fifth Ice Age is the one we're in now. It's called the Quaternary Ice Age and it has been going on for 2.5 million years. The coldest phase of this Ice Age has already peaked about 20,000 years ago when Canada was covered with ice. At the peak of this Ice Age, the ice was more than 12,000 feet in thickness not only across Canada, but also across Russia and as far south as the continent of South America.

Maximum glaciation of the northern hemisphere during the Quaternary climatic cycles.

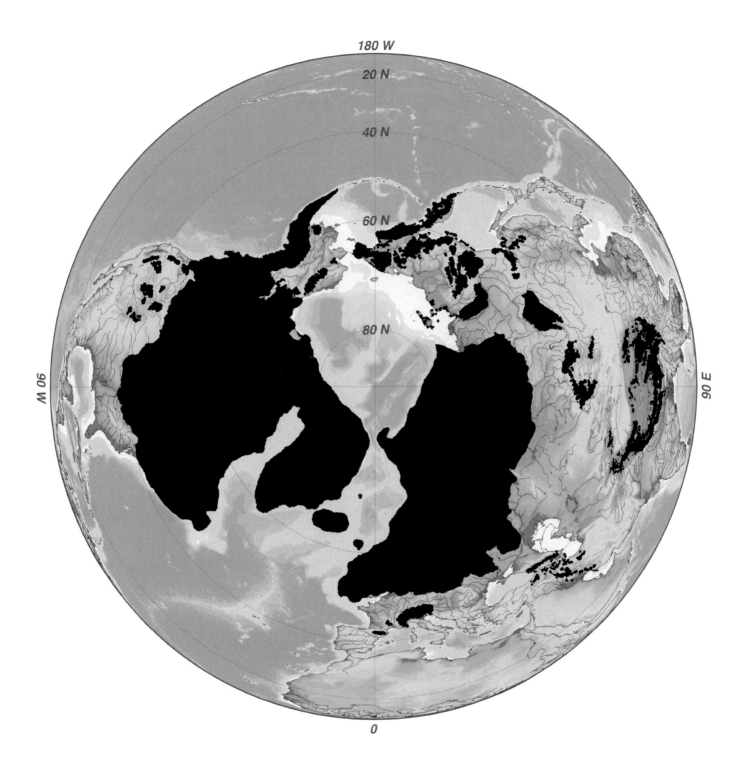

Sea levels across the world decreased by as much as 400 feet. The overall average temperature around the world dipped down 10 degrees Fahrenheit. In some regions of the world it dipped down about 40 degrees Fahrenheit. The Gulf Coast states of what is now the United States had pine forests and there were prairie grasses that were like the vegetation in the Northeast and Canada.

Glacial grooves in granite bedrock, legacy of the ice age..

We're currently in a warmer interglacial phase called the Holocene period, but we're still in the Quaternary Ice Age.

Glacier crevasses in Norway, Jostedalsbreen

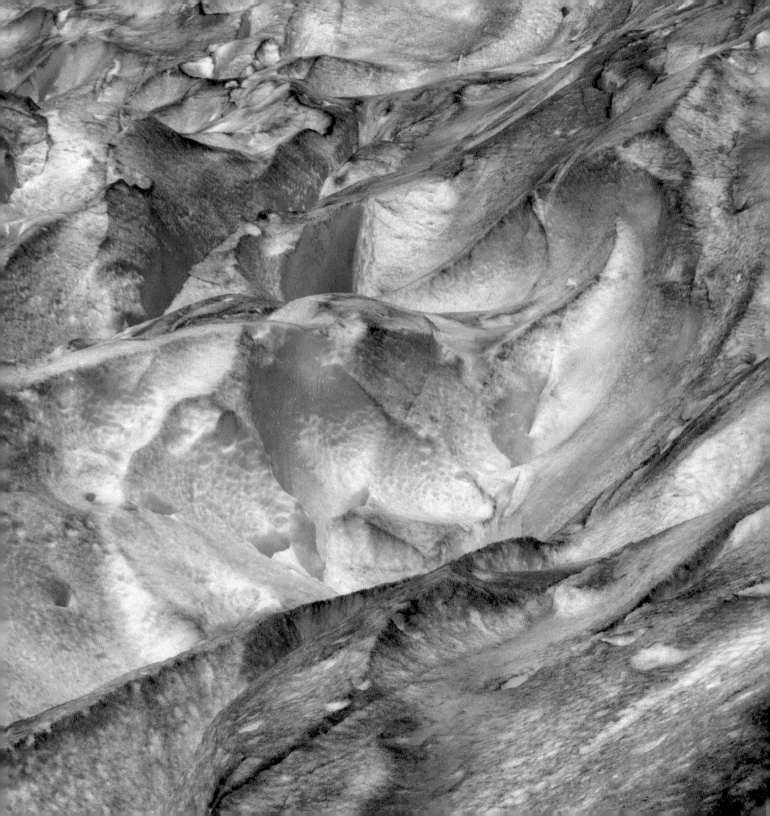

HOW DO SCIENTISTS KNOW ABOUT PAST ICE AGES?

Except for the Ice Age we're in now, the other Ice Ages were millions of years ago. It took a long time for scientists to piece together the clues that explained how Earth's temperatures fluctuated to create Ice Ages. Hundreds of years ago, people in Europe noticed that the glaciers located in the Alps had decreased in size. They began to wonder about the expansion and contraction of glaciers and the types of climate changes that caused that cycle.

Grossglockner II

Some scientists in the 19th century believed that the wooly mammoth and saber-toothed cat were killed off by huge floods. Louis Agassiz, a geologist from Switzerland, began studying the aftereffects of glaciers that remained after a severe *"Global Winter."* He was convinced that climate changes had caused the animals to die out. Later evidence verified his findings.

Two mammoth in a field covered with snow.

In 1941, the mathematician Milutin Milankovitch from Serbia made painstaking calculations to show the fluctuations in temperatures around the world for a time span of 600,000 years. He cross referenced the orbit of the Earth as well as the tilt of its axis to explain the astronomical variations that might cause a shift in Earth's temperature.

Franz Josef glacier in New Zealand.

WHAT CAUSES ICE AGES?

There are many factors that have the potential to start an Ice Age. These factors sometimes happen at the same time. When the global temperature shifts enough to cause an Ice Age, it isn't a quick shift. The shift takes millions of years one way or the other, either warmer or colder.

THE ORBIT OF THE EARTH

The Earth isn't always the same distance from the Sun. Every 100,000 years or thereabouts Earth's orbit changes to slightly more elliptical instead of more circular. These changes in the Earth's orbit over very long periods of time are called the *Milankovitch Cycles*. When the Earth is farther from the Sun, the temperature of Earth's surface and its atmosphere get colder. The difference in temperature can jump start an Ice Age.

Milankovich cycle.

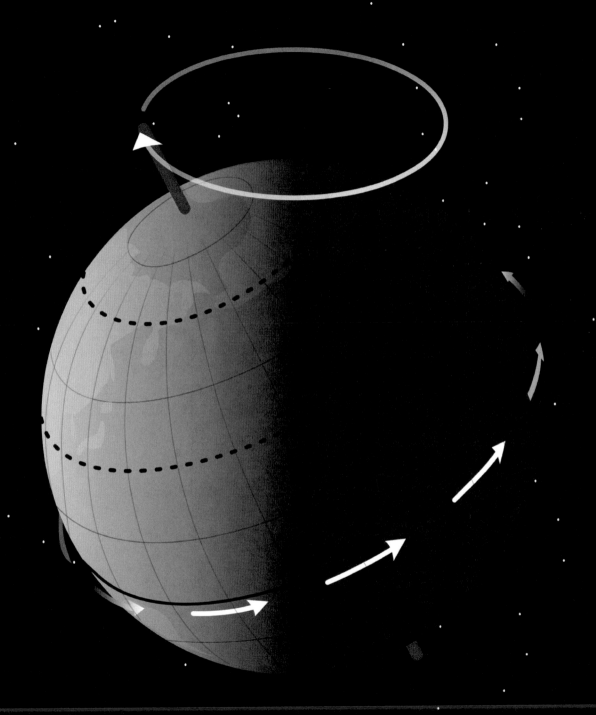

THE OUTPUT OF THE SUN

Sometimes our Sun puts out more energy than at other times. When the Sun has a cycle of lower energy, it doesn't create as much warmth over a span of millions of years and this can cause an Ice Age.

Abstract space sunrise.

THE CONDITION OF THE ATMOSPHERE

When there's not much volcanic activity worldwide, it can cause the level of carbon dioxide to decrease to the point where the atmospheric temperatures cool. If the global temperature decreases, even just a small amount over a long period of time, it can cause an Ice Age.

South Pole Expedition.

Once there is ice and snow over large areas of land, the Sun's rays as well as its energy are reflected, which lowers the temperature further.

Holtanna Peak.

The opposite happens as well. When there is a saturation of carbon dioxide in the atmosphere either from natural volcanic activity or pollution that causes greenhouse gases, the temperature warms. Greenhouse gases hold heat in the atmosphere, which over time can end an Ice Age.

Winter view on eruption Klyuchevskaya Sopka.

The current increase in greenhouse gases from manmade pollution has scientists concerned. Depending on the shift in temperature, global warming could be devastating to the climate on Earth.

THE MOVEMENT OF OCEAN CURRENTS

Changes in the currents of our oceans can also cause an Ice Age, especially if the number of ice sheets are increasing worldwide.

Awesome! Now you know more about the Ice Ages on Earth and what causes them. You can find more Environment books from Baby Professor by searching the website of your favorite book retailer.

Visit

BABY PROFESSOR
EDUCATION KIDS

www.BabyProfessorBooks.com

to download Free Baby Professor eBooks
and view our catalog of new and exciting
Children's Books

Made in the USA
Monee, IL
09 July 2024